6-02

Rare Treasure

Mary Anning and Her Remarkable Discoveries

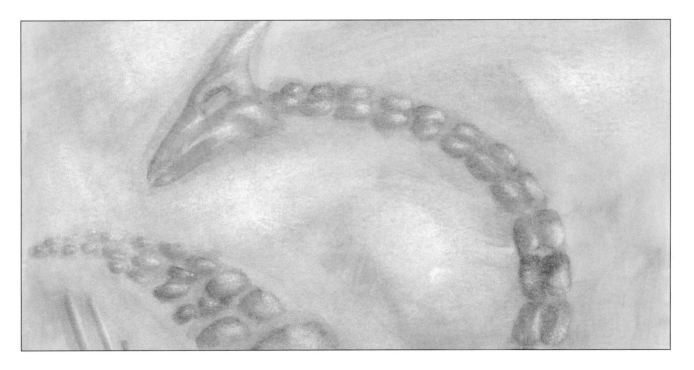

Written and Illustrated by **Don Brown**

Houghton Mifflin Company Boston 1999

With special thanks to Hugh Torrens
for his generous advice and assistance,
and the people of the British Museum of Natural History
and Dorset County Library for their kindness and aid.

The text of this book is set in 14-point Goudy.
The illustrations are pen and ink and watercolor on paper.

Library of Congress Cataloging-in-Publication Data
Brown, Don, 1949–
Rare treasure : Mary Anning and her remarkable discoveries /
written and illustrated by Don Brown.
p.   cm.
Summary: Describes the life of the English girl whose discovery of
an Ichthyosaurus fossil led to a lasting interest in other prehistoric animals.
ISBN 0-395-92286-0
1. Anning Mary, 1799–1847 — Juvenile literature. 2. Women paleontologists —
England — Biography — Juvenile literature. 3. Ichthyosaurus — Juvenile literature.
[1. Anning, Mary, 1799–1847. 2. Paleontologists. 3. Women — Biography. 4. Fossils.] I. Title.
QE707.A56B76   1999
560'.92 — dc21   98-32372   CIP AC

Manufactured in the United States of America
BVG 10 9 8 7 6 5 4 3 2 1

For Rita-Rita, my own Rare Treasure

IN 1799, Mary Anning was born in Lyme Regis, a small English port tucked tightly between cliffs and coast.

Mary was poor and her life was hard—as hard as stone.
But she was also curious and smart and her spirit shone—it shone like a gem.

Mary's life started with a bang—the bang of thunder. Infant Mary was outdoors with her nursemaid when a sudden and terrible storm burst. The nursemaid grabbed Mary and, with two other young women, raced to the cover of a nearby elm. The sky exploded and lightning struck the tree!

Only Mary survived.

It was a miraculous escape. When Mary blossomed into a lively and intelligent child, some townspeople said the lightning had made her that way.

Mary and her older brother, Joseph, were just a few years old when they began
visiting the nearby rocky beaches with their father. Richard Anning taught them
how to hunt for fossils.

Fossils were strange and mysterious. Although they had been found before, scientists were just beginning to understand that they were the remains of animals or plants that no longer existed, living things that had died many, many years ago.

Usually the remains of plants and animals decompose or are eaten, but sometimes they are covered by dirt or sink in mud. Of these, a rare few lie undisturbed for millions of years. While they are buried, the soft parts, such as flesh, decay, leaving bones, shell, or flat impressions in the earth. Minerals seep into these remains and become stone. These fossils survive hidden in the ground until they are revealed by a shovel or pick, are driven to the surface by an earthquake or volcano, or are uncovered when wind or water wears away the earth.

The Annings displayed the puzzling yet delightful fossils that they found on a table near Richard's shop on Bridge Street. Wealthy tourists visiting the popular Lyme Regis shore bought them.

The family struggled to survive on the earnings of Richard's carpentry work, and the extra money they earned by selling fossils helped. Then Mary's father died and the family was thrown into bitter poverty.

Mary and Joseph still collected and sold fossils they found on the rugged ribbon of shore that separated the sea and the cliffs.

One day Joseph found a fantastic fossil skull. It was nearly the length of a man's arm and had a long snout that held many sharp teeth.

Was it a crocodile? A dragon? A monster?
What did the *rest* of the creature look like?

A year passed before Mary discovered the answer.

In 1811, Mary found a fossilized skeleton beneath a cliff called Black Ven, where Joseph had found the skull. It looked like a porpoise and was about seven feet long.

Men helped her free the skeleton from the earth. She sold it to a rich neighbor, who showed it to scientists. They were thrilled by the rare treasure, a fossil of a reptile that had once lived in the sea. The scientists called the creature ichthyosaur, which means fish lizard. Only a few ichthyosaur fossils had ever been found and none were as nearly perfect as this one.

Almost everyone forgot that it had been found by twelve-year-old Mary Anning and her teenage brother.

ichthyosaur

Mary still collected fossils and also earned money from small jobs she did for her neighbors. One of them, Mrs. Stock, gave her a geology book. From it Mary learned about rocks and mountains and the earth. She read other books and taught herself about animals, fish, and fossils.

Years passed. When Mary was twenty years old, she and her mother and brother were still living together. They remained very poor and even sold their furniture to pay their rent.

Joseph became an upholsterer and Mary collected fossils alone. She made it her life's work.

It also must have been Mary's great delight because she pursued it despite the dangers on the rocky shore. Boulders fell from the cliffs, torrents of thick black mud slid down from the heights, high seas pummeled the shore, and waves could sweep a careless visitor away. But the beach was rich in fossils. As the cliffs crumbled, new fossils were revealed. Many were smaller than your thumb. Others were yards long and embedded in thick, heavy rock. Workers were needed to dig them from the earth, and then horses carted them away.

Mary sold her treasures from a small, cluttered shop on Broad Street. There she freed her latest discoveries from dirt, sand, and rock. Mary worked very carefully, sometimes for days, to avoid damaging the fossils. Sometimes she cemented a fossil to a frame to help support it. She drew pictures of them. She studied her science books.

In 1823, Mary discovered the first complete fossil of a plesiosaur, another reptile that had lived in the sea. It was an astonishing nine-foot-long creature with a long, serpentlike neck, a lizard's head, a crocodile's teeth, a chameleon's ribs, and the paddles of a whale.

plesiosaur

The discovery excited scientists. Like Mary's earlier find, the ichthyosaur fossil, it was a rare clue to solving the puzzle of life long ago. What creature had become this jumble of bones trapped in rock? How did it move? What did it eat? How was it like modern creatures? Answering these questions helped reveal the ancient world in which the plesiosaur had lived.

Mary Anning's fame grew as people learned that she was an extraordinary fossil collector and a talented scientist. People followed her on fossil hunts. Together they plodded over the rough rocks, waded knee-deep in water, and scrambled up the cliffs to avoid the crashing waves.

Once Mary had to rescue a teenager, Anna Maria Pinney, from rough water. Pinney said Mary carried her with the "same ease as you would a baby."

William Buckland, a famous geologist, brought his family to Lyme Regis to meet Mary and to search for fossils. She escorted Buckland and his children on fossil hunts. Richard Owens, the scientist who invented the word *dinosaur*, also combed the beach with Mary.

Day after day, Mary searched in the shadows of the treacherous cliffs, sometimes walking ten miles in one day. Her sharp eyes spotted fossils where others saw nothing. Mary's dog trotted faithfully beside her. People said the dog guarded her discoveries while she fetched her tools or got help.

During one hunt, part of a cliff collapsed. Heavy rocks crashed at Mary's feet and nearly crushed her.

Another time, Mary found a large fossil. She and a helper labored to recover it. The hard work blinded Mary to the rising tide that flooded the beach. Waves drenched the pair, but they saved the treasure. Later, Mary asked the man why he hadn't warned her of the rapidly flowing tide. "I was ashamed to say I was frightened when you didn't regard it," he replied.

In 1828, Mary discovered a very rare fossil of a pterodactyl, a flying reptile that had the body of a lizard and the snout of a crocodile. Mary's pterodactyl was displayed at the British Natural History Museum and is still there today.

Mary tried to make *sense* of her discoveries. She read her science books and studied her collection. Mary shared her ideas with the finest scientists. They prized the thoughts of the remarkable young woman who had left school when she was eleven.

It was said, "She knows more about the science than anyone else."

By 1836, Mary had found the fossils of three ichthyosaurs, two plesiosaurs, a pterodactyl, a strange sharklike fish called *Squaloraja,* and an untold number of small or incomplete fossils.

Mary's fossil shop on Broad Street was now crowded with customers.

One visitor wished to record the name of the woman who had asssembled such a wonderful collection. With a firm hand, Mary wrote her name in the man's notebook.

"I am well known throughout the whole of Europe," she said proudly.

Mary Anning lived from 1799 to 1847, but her spirit dwelled in a time millions of years ago, when the monsters and dragons we now call dinosaurs roamed.

She had little money, but she was rich in spirit.

She was unschooled, but the professors heeded her words.

She rarely strayed from her home, but her name became known everywhere.

Mary Anning pried fossils from the ground, but it was knowledge that she unearthed.